Old Broughton, Drumelzier, Manor, Stobo and Tweedsmuir
Ann Matheson

This part of Broughton was until the late 19th century a separate settlement known as Calzeat. The parish church is the focal point, but its spire no longer points heavenward, having been removed in the early 1990s for safety reasons. The building on the extreme right of the picture was the Free Church school and schoolhouse, which were next door to the Free Church. Between the schoolhouse and the parish church is Calzeat Farm. The parish church was built here when Broughton, Glenholm and Kilbucho parishes were united in 1794. The earlier church, dedicated to St. Maurice, was at the north end of the village, an ancient religious site dating from at least the 12th century. Beside it, there is a beautifully restored cell, which tradition describes as that of St. Llolan, one of St. Ninian's bishops, but it may just be the vault of a local laird. The third minister of the new church, from 1813 until 1854, was the Rev Hamilton Paul. Born in Ayrshire, he was a friend of Robert Burns and one of the nine men who met for the first recorded 'Burns Supper' in 1801. He is credited with saving the 'Auld Brig o Doon', by writing a petition and circulating it all over Scotland. His wit is evident in this extract from the petition:

'Let Nanny's sark and Maggie's mangled tail
Plead in my cause and in the cause prevail'

He was noted for humour, hospitality and, with a crow and a monkey as household pets, his mild eccentricity.

The ancient families of Tweedsmuir are the Frasers of Oliver and Fruid. These Frasers were of Norman origin and lived at Fruid until the end of the 16th century. Menzion was part of their barony. A branch of the family also built Oliver Castle, long since gone. Simon Fraser was a distant relative of William Wallace. He fought with him and, like him, was hanged, drawn and quartered in London in 1306. The Fruid Valley is rich in prehistory. North-east of Menzion farmhouse, the road passes between 3 standing stones, one of which is known as 'The Giant's Stone'. In 2006, Biggar archaeologists uncovered the sites of two Bronze Age roundhouses, now below the high water mark in Fruid Reservoir, which was opened in 1968 to supplement the water supply from Talla. The site of Fruid Castle, which was thought to precede Oliver Castle, also lies beneath the reservoir.

© Ann Matheson, 2014
First published in the United Kingdom, 2014,
by Stenlake Publishing Ltd.
www.stenlake.co.uk
ISBN 9781840336719

The publishers regret that they cannot supply copies of any pictures featured in this book.

Acknowledgements

Tam Ward, Biggar Archaeology Group, Ian Hamilton, Liz Hamilton, Linda Lewin, Peter McGillivray, Jenni Watt, Stobo Health Spa, Douglas Hind, Caledonian Railway Association

Further Reading

The books listed below were used by the author during his research. None are available from Stenlake Publishing; please contact your local bookshop or reference library.

Life and Times in the Upper Tweed valley, compiled by Margaret Railton from journals left by Andrew Lorimer
Peeblesshire newspaper, 8 Jan 1982
Historic Haunts of Peeblesshire : Gilbert Rae
History of Peeblesshire, J.W. Buchan and Rev H Paton
Peeblesshire, The Royal Commission on the Ancient and Historical Monuments of Scotland
Origines parochiales Scotiae
History of the Celtic Place Names of Scotland, W.J. Watson
The History of Stobo and the Castle, Stobo Health Spa pamphlet
Biggar Archaeology Group, various reports
Broughton Free Kirk and thereabouts 1843-1943, Rev David Marshall Forrester
The Kirk in the midst, Andrew Fox
Companion to Tweed, George Burnett
Annals of a Tweeddale Parish, Andrew Baird
AJB HOPE personal website
Millennium Memories, C. Brown and M. Taylor
Horae Subsecivae, Dr John Brown

Introduction

The Upper Tweed Valley guards its secrets. Those who wish to discover them must venture from the main road into the tributary valleys. There, clues are scattered all over the brooding landscape, waiting to be recognised, interpreted and woven into a vibrant and colourful tapestry of the past.

The main valley carved out by the River Tweed was widened and deepened by the glaciers of the last Ice Age, making it flat-floored and steep-sided. The hills, dissected by the tributary valleys, have been 'sandpapered' by the same ice, making them smooth and rounded rather than sharply dramatic.

People have lived here since the Stone Age, most of the hammers, flints and axeheads they left behind now part of the National Museum's collection. Everywhere, there is evidence of Bronze Age people, their platform sites, cairns and cists, the burnt mounds where they heated water using hot stones. In turn, the low hills surrounded by marshy valleys provided excellent defensive sites for Iron Age people, whose cultivation terraces can still be seen on the slopes, e.g. at Kingledores and Drumelzier. These Celtic-Brythonic people have also left a legacy in place names like the Logan Water, Dreva, Kilbucho or Tinnis. The Romans have no role in this history, having chosen to penetrate Central Scotland via the Clyde Valley rather than the Tweed.

After the Norman Conquest of England in 1066, many Normans and Flemings drifted north to be given land by the king in return for military support. The first mention of Broughton is in church records of 1175, when the Norman, Ralph Le Neym, gifted half a ploughgate of land (52 acres) to the 'chapel of Broctun.'

Among the many overlords who followed him, two at least attained some notoriety. The first of these was John Murray, a staunch supporter of Bonnie Prince Charlie and, as the Scottish correspondent to Rome, the main link between Charles Edward Stuart and the Scottish Jacobites. His wife apparently was equally ardent. She appeared at the cross in Edinburgh, on horseback, adorned with white ribbons and a white cockade with a drawn sword in her hand to proclaim her loyalty to the Stuart cause. Murray was with Charles through most of the '45 rebellion, but had to return home to his sister's house at Polmood, where he was captured by the dragoons and taken to London. There, he turned king's evidence to save his own skin. For this treachery, he was held in contempt and nicknamed 'Evidence Murray'.

There is a story of Sir Walter Scott's father allegedly throwing a cup out of the window because Murray had drunk from it, saying, 'Neither lip of me nor of mine comes after Murray of Broughton's'. Murray lived on mostly in London and, in 1771, his sons placed him in a lunatic asylum where he died shortly after.

The second notorious laird was Robert McQueen, Lord Braxfield, who was the character source for the 'Hanging Judge' in Robert Louis Stevenson's unfinished novel, *Weir of Hermiston*. He stubbornly used Scots, the last judge to do so, despite the Anglicisation that had followed the Union of the Parliaments in 1707. He purchased the Broughton estates c. 1780 and they were held by his descendants until 1921. One of his most famous quotes was, 'Ye're a gey clever chiel, but ye'll be nane the waur o a hangin''

A nostalgic plume of smoke follows the train north-east across the Tweed Valley floor towards Broughton c. 1912. For most of this part of the route onward to Biggar, the line is built on embankments to keep it above flood water. This is a particularly boggy stretch of land, the eastern end of the Biggar gap, which was once occupied by a much larger river, the ancient Tweed.

The message on the back of the PC, from a Yorkshire visitor, reflects the new wave of tourism: 'Spending the weekend here. Isn't it pretty? England can't come up to it'.

Defence has always been a priority in the Borderlands, which for centuries were vulnerable to attacks from both the English and from cattle reivers on both sides of the national boundary. In 1537, the Scottish Parliament decreed that every major Border landowner should build a barmkyn (stone enclosure) for defence against the English in the troubled years after Flodden. Lesser lairds had to build wooden enclosures or peels, which later gave their name to the towers themselves. Such towers were built along the whole length of the Tweed from its source to Berwick. This part of the valley had peel houses at Hawkshaw, Fruid, Oliver, Polmood, Kingledores, Mossfennan, Wrae, Quarter, Stanhope, Drumelzier, Tinnis, Dreva, Stobo, Dawyck, carefully located so that beacon warnings could be transmitted along the line. In 1872, the records of the Highland Society noted that Drumelzier was the last in a chain of fortresses along the Tweed and that they were all gone. In the Manor Valley, there are the ruins of at least six towers and six peel houses. Defence was paramount as the main route of the cattle rustlers was along the Thief's Road which followed the watershed between the two valleys.

Many famous and infamous families lived in these secluded valleys, among them the Frasers whose beautiful daughter was the reason for a feud between the Tweedies and the neighbouring Flemings; a feud which caused the murder of John, Lord Fleming, in 1524. Another long-standing feud between the Tweedies and the Veitches of Dawyck was not settled until James Tweedie was killed in a one-to-one fight, after the king himself had intervened in 1611 to try to put a stop to the continuous violence.

Farther east in Peeblesshire, Sir Walter Scott has romanticised the Borders, but this landscape too nurtured and inspired men and women of literary fame; James Hogg, Robert Burns, Walter Scott himself and John Buchan, as well as his sister who wrote under the name O. Douglas.

And this is a place of legends. Who was the Merlin whose grave allegedly lies beneath a thorn bush in Drumelzier? Who was the lady of Mossfennan whom three suitors found to be less than beautiful? And did the Black Dwarf of the Manor Valley possess supernatural powers or was he the victim of disease and poverty?

In modern times, the Upper Tweed has become almost exclusively sheep farming territory (though few ewes are now milked for cheese production!), while its steep valleys have been flooded to provide water for Edinburgh and their slopes often planted with commercial forests. The villages, which once were self-sufficient, are now dormitory settlements with few services, but they retain a strong community spirit. Tourism and recreation are discreet: Dawyck Gardens with their eclectic collection of international trees, the Glenholm centre, the Beechgrove Garden and the John Buchan Way, opened in 2003, which provides walkers with a guided, albeit strenuous, route across the hills from Broughton to Peebles. Fishing in the Tweed's unpolluted water has always been a popular pastime and the opportunities for hill-walking are endless.

Still, the secret landscape waits. Few passing travellers know of the drama of its prehistory, Merlin's grave, the ill-fated ruins of Tinnis Castle, the ancient mother church at Stobo, the exotic trees of Dawyck, the 17th and 18th century sheep buchts (open-ended pens for milking sheep), some close by old shieling huts which farmers of the period would have used for transhumance, the quiet graves of the men who died in the building of the Talla Reservoir and its railway. Shades of monks, hermits, border reivers, Covenanters, traitors, Jacobites and warring families stalk the valleys.

The area has enormous tourist potential, but it is to be hoped that the upper Tweed will continue to keep its secrets, divulging them only to those who make the effort to discover them

Trout fishing has always been a popular pastime in the upper Tweed. In the 19th century, the fishing was one of the main attractions of a stay at the Crook Inn.
'Angle here, or angle there,
Troots are soomin' ilkawhere.'
These are the words of the 19th century 'angler-bard', Thomas Tod Stoddart.

The picture dates from *c.* 1910. The school (right) and the schoolmaster's house look very similar today. Inside the school, there was one classroom with tiered rows of desks and a fireplace at each end where children who had walked long distances could dry off their wet clothes. Sheep fat, butter or tar was used to give their boots a waterproof coating and old stockings, minus the feet, called 'hoggers' were pulled over the boots to keep out the snow. In an area where most people were employed in sheep farming, knitting was an important subject in the curriculum. Both boys and girls learned how to knit and most shepherds knitted socks as they walked over the hills inspecting their flocks. Tweedsmuir mutton was very popular in the north of England and a large percentage of fleeces went to Yorkshire woollen mills. In the early 20th century, there were schools at Broughton, Drumelzier, Kilbucho, Glenholm, Skirling and Tweedsmuir.

The 'wee school' at Tweedhopefoot, probably the smallest in Scotland and sometimes called 'the academy', was opened in the 1890s to cater for children too far away to attend Tweedsmuir. It served the community for about 40 years until 1938-9 and the picture dates from *c.* 1900. This green corrugated iron hut contained a single room that could accommodate 10-12 children. There was no running water and the toilet was a spar over the burn, with a small wooden hut above it. Children walked several miles to attend school, although winter weather often made their journey impossible. They had a broad curriculum of English, history, geography, music, religious education and crafts. One notable headmaster was was Mr John Yellowlees whose daughter Janet helped out, teaching knitting and sewing. The wee school is preserved, still with five desks, a stand of faded books and magazines, the old metal stove: but the inkwells are empty even although the teacher's coat still hangs on a peg by the door. This interesting extract from the *Brisbane Courier*, dated 27 Nov 1929, shows that news of the wee school spread to the other side of the world. 'Among the lonely Peeblesshire hills, near the source of the Tweed, is a little corrugated iron hut, measuring 4 by 3 yards. This Is Tweedhopefoot School, which the Peeblesshire Authority have Just, after due consideration, decided to keep open. It seats 12 pupils, but at present only six attend. The youngest, six years of age, has to walk over three miles to school.'

A family goes for a walk in Tweedsmuir in the 1920s. The path, which was a short cut from the village to the old post office, is still there. Burnt mounds, cairns, platform sites and standing stones provide evidence that people have lived in this area at least since the Bronze Age. Over 100 of these sites have been damaged by forestry plantations.

The 'Post Office' sign can just be seen on the right hand side of the picture. It has been there at least since 1896. In the 1901 census, Agnes Currie was the post office clerk. Her father and brother were both tailors and the family address in the 1901 census was 'Left Bank of Tweed Newbigging'. Ten years before that, 18-year-old Mary Ann Tod was a post runner, possibly for the postal service then operated by the Crook Inn. In 1831, both the driver and the guard of the Dumfries Edinburgh mail coach lost their lives in snow drifts on the old Edinburgh-Dumfries road, east of the present A701. After the horses had foundered in the snow, the men cut them loose and attempted to go well beyond the call of duty by delivering the mailbags on foot to Tweedshaws Inn, a halfway house between Moffat and the Crook Inn. A sturdy sandstone monument off the A701, just south of the Peeblesshire border, commemorates their valiant determination.

Tweedsmuir Church, in this almost-Gothic landsape, was built in 1874, replacing an earlier church built in 1648. Leaning against the north-west corner of the church, there is a weathered stone slab, carved with a shield and cartouche. This may be a relic of the older church or of a vault associated with it. The church bell, dated 1773, came from the earlier church. The church sits on a mound called Quarter Knowe, where skeletons were found when the foundations of the earlier church were being dug in the 1620s-30s, indicating that an even older church probably stood there. The present building was designed by John Lessels, a famous Edinburgh architect. It is built of whinstone, with a red sandstone broach spire (i.e. the spire rises from a tower). It has several impressive stained glass windows and a war memorial made from an oak tree which was planted by Sir Walter Scott at Abbotsford.

Here lyes John Hunter Martyr who was cruely Murdered at Corehead by Col James Douglas and his party for his Adherance To the Word of God and Scotland's Covenanted Work of Reformation 1685 Erected in the year 1726.

Reverse side: *when Zions King was robbed of his right His witnesses in Scotland put to flight: When popish prelats & Indulgancie combin'd 'gainst Christ to Ruine presbytrie, All who would not unto their idols bow They socht them out & and who they found they slew For owning of Christ's cause I then did die My blood for vengeance on His en'mies did cry.*

The "Covenanter's Stone", erected in 1726, commemorates John Hunter, killed in 1685. According to Andrew Lorimer, children had to recite these words when the minister visited the school. John Hunter had been visiting a sick friend at Corehead, when he was surprised by Colonel James Douglas and his dragoons, who pursued and shot him, then threw his body over a cliff at the Devil's Beef Tub.

The Crook, one of the oldest inns in Scotland, received its first licence in 1604. It is mentioned in a document, dated 1621, when a messenger was despatched from Edinburgh to arrest Sir Patrick Porteous of Hawkshaw for debt. When they stopped at the Crook for refreshment, Porteous's neighbours rescued him! Perhaps its most famous patrons were Robert Burns and Sir Walter Scott.

Willie Wastle's Bar in the Crook Inn was added at the same time as the Art Deco extension (see the back cover).

She has an e'e - she has but ane,
The cat has twa the very colour,
Five rusty teeth, forbye a stump,
A clapper-tongue wad deave a miller;
A whiskin beard about her mou,
Her nose and chin they threaten ither:
Sic a wife as Willie had,
I wad na gie a button for her.

Just north of Tweedsmuir on the A701, a signpost marks the 'SITE OF LINKUMDODDIE' where, according to Burns's politically incorrect poem, lived Willie Wastle and his aesthetically challenged wife. The lady who inspired the poem was actually the wife of a farmer near Ellisland, near Dumfries, where Burns lived from 1788-91. Burns was said to have written the poem in the kitchen of the Crook Inn where he stayed several times when travelling from Dumfries to Edinburgh. The poem is displayed on a mural in the inn.

Talla Water joins the Tweed north of Tweedsmuir village. In the 1890s, Talla was sold by the Trustees of the Earl of Wemyss and March to Edinburgh and District Water Board. Here, work is in progress, beneath the Renaissance-style Victoria Lodge, built as the Board's headquarters. Work began in 1885 to build a railway line from Broughton Station to transport raw materials and workers to the site. From Carluke, 100,000 tons of puddle clay went to make the dam trench impermeable. The clay was transported from the railhead by an overhead rope, nicknamed a 'Blondin', after the famous Blondin who carried people across the Niagara gorge on a tightrope. James Young & Sons of Edinburgh were contracted to build the railway from Rachan. However, when 14 clay-filled wagons were derailed at Broughton in September 1899, causing huge delays, the Caledonian Railway manager banned the Young engine from the line until it had been overhauled. When Young's company went into liquidation a week later, the contract went to John Best of Leith. Best built a wooden platform close to the Crook Inn, where he also had a financial interest. He claimed he paid the workers on Fridays and got his money back on Mondays!

These two pictures, featuring the building of the overflow, show the scale of the work in progress. Note the keystones in both pictures and the cloud of steam in the second one. All the cranes and shovels were steam-driven. Some of the workers, mostly Irish labourers, can be seen. The 1901 census records over 200 men, women and children crammed into four large huts, each housing 40-60 navvies, and eight smaller ones, which were largely occupied by skilled workers and their families. The groups of huts were named after local landmarks, e.g. Logan Burn, Wrae, Mossfennan, Stirkfield. Not surprisingly, disease spread rapidly in these cramped conditions and in 1902-3, an outbreak of smallpox in Central Scotland was traced to the Talla works. In 1903, the British Medical Journal reported that ten cases had been noted there in that month. Over thirty people died during the construction work, only a few of these from the smallpox epidemic. In Tweedsmuir, a grave stretches the width of the churchyard. Above it, the memorial reads, *'To the memory of the men who died during the progress of Talla Water Works, 1895-1905, of whom over thirty are interred in this churchyard. Erected by their fellow workers and others.'*

Following the valve-opening ceremony, when Talla Water was diverted into the reservoir bed, the reservoir was declared open on September 28th, 1905. Two special trains brought guests. The photograph shows the marquees in the background, set up for their entertainment. Sir Walter Thorburn, a well known Border tweed merchant, made a speech in which he expressed the hope that the supply railway would remain, as it was so convenient for the people who lived there. Alas, as soon as the job was done, Best removed his locomotives. Several approaches were made to the Caledonian Railway Company, but to no avail. In 1910, the railway materials were sold and by July 1912, the last piece of track was lifted. The water is carried to Edinburgh by a 22 mile long aqueduct and iron pipes.

The reservoir is complete. Today the valley sides are forested and ospreys can be seen fishing. Victoria Lodge is now a guest-house. At the head of the reservoir, the Talla still tumbles down over dramatic rocky crags, described by Sir Walter Scott in *The Heart of Midlothian*, as the site of a Covenanting conventicle held in 1682

'A small river, or rather a mountain torrent, called the Talla, breaks down the glen with great fury, dashing successively over a number of small cascades, which has procured the spot the name of Talla Linns'. Sir Walter Scott's source of information was *Faithful Contendings displayed* by Michael Shiels, an account of the meetings of hard line Covenanters in the 1680s. The meeting at Talla had broken up in furious dispute about the types of taxes that should or should not be paid. Immediately after the meeting, a report of it was sent by the curate at Tweedsmuir to the council at Edinburgh who immediately issued a proclamation against all who had convened there (about 80) warning the people not to supply them with any kind of refuge or food and commanding the bailiffs and sheriffs to search them out and arrest them. The diligence of these officers apparently caused great distress to the local people suspected of giving shelter to any of the Covenanters who had attended the conventicle.

There is a tradition which claims that the Polmood lands, along the north side of the Polmood Burn, were gifted to Norman Hunter by King Malcolm Canmore in 1057, but there are no records to verify this claim. There are records, however, which indicate that Polmood was under the barony of Oliver Castle and that generations of the Hunter family lived there from the 15th century until the late 18th century. When the last of the old line died, several claimants made unsuccessful bids to claim the estate, resulting in a law suit which went on for over 30 years. Polmood was in ruins by 1864, when it was rebuilt by Houston Mitchell, who had made his fortune in Australia and Jamaica. A stone from the earlier house, built into the eastern gable wall, is carved with the initials R H, Richard Hunter who died in 1689, and beneath the kitchen floor, the vaulted cellar of the old house remains.

Broughton village street looking north, early 1900s. This part of Broughton is known simply as 'the village'. At the far end of the terrace (left) was the old school. An article in *The Peeblesshire News* (1982) recalls that the nearby village shop had wooden shelves, carved with graffiti, that looked like made-over school desks. The school was transformed into the village police station in the early 20th century. The two-storey building (left) is 'The Green' which, as a staging post on the Edinburgh-Dumfries road, was the focal point of the village. The mail coach from Edinburgh to Carlisle arrived daily at 1 a.m. and the coach from Moffat at a more civilised hour, about mid-day. The groom occupied the room above the kitchen, where he could look out for the coaches arriving. From the early 1850s until the 1880s, John Masterton and his family lived at Broughton Green, the farm steading at the corner of the Dreva Road. In 1921, when the Broughton estate was dispersed, the three Masterton brothers bought the inn. Helen, their sister, married the Rev John Buchan, who had been preaching as a locum in Broughton Free Church. Their son, born in 1875, was John Buchan, the famous novelist and statesman. The hens in the picture recall Meg Lorimer, housekeeper at The Green, who looked after her cows and hens across the street. When it was feeding time for the hens, they gathered round The Green's kitchen door to remind her.

Broughton village street looking south. In 1793, Broughton consisted of 20 houses containing 36 adults and 61 children. Twelve farms employed 28 male and 23 female farm servants. There were four weavers, four wrights, one tailor, one smith, one miller, two shoemakers, three shopkeepers, 200 black cattle and over 2000 sheep; in short, a typical Southern Upland village. The village itself 'was remarked by passengers for its neatness.' The *Statistical Account* of 1834 describes the annual October fairs held in the village street, 'with stalls overloaded with produce and merchandise'. By that time, it had become a hiring fair, where also butter and cheese prices were fixed for the next year.

Greenmantle Hotel and Springwellbrae.

The Greenmantle Hotel had a short life. Built in 1961, it closed in 2001 and was demolished to make way for ten new houses. Built on land that had belonged to the Buchan family, the hotel was named after John Buchan's famous novel, *Greenmantle*.

The Disruption of 1843 saw many members of Broughton, Drumelzier and Stobo congregations leave the established church. The new Free Church congregation met for a while in a barn at Rachan Mill before their new church was built that same year. The first sermon was preached by Rev Dr Thomas Chalmers, the founder of the Free Church of Scotland. Its first minister was William Welsh who remained for 50 years. He married Christina Guthrie whose father founded the Guthrie schools in Edinburgh. The Free Church (behind the white fence, left) closed in 1978, to reopen, in 1983, as the John Buchan Centre, which sadly had to be relocated in Peebles in 2012.

Broughton Place, built in 1938 in the style of a 17th century Scottish tower house, was designed by the architect Basil Spence. It was built on the site of an earlier house which had belonged to the notorious Secretary Murray of Broughton (see page 3) whose house was burned to the ground in 1773. Although Basil Spence had originally intended to build it in stone, financial constraints resulted in its being brick-built and harled, with stone used only for details. Inside, wood panelling and decorative plaster ceilings extend the pseudo 17th century ambience and the sculptor Hew Lorimer was commissioned to create a pair of relief panels and lion gateposts. The house was commissioned by Professor Thomas and Mrs Martha Elliott, whose main residence was in Chelsea, as Thomas was professor of Medicine at University College, London. *Inset*: Martha Mc Cosh, wife of Professor Elliot, in First World War Red Cross uniform. The house was later converted into flats with an art gallery on the ground floor.

Left: Little has changed, except for the horse and cart, since this postcard was printed in 1911, when this ford was a route from the main road to Drumelzier just over a mile away to the north-east. Evidence of ancient man can also be found here in the remains of old settlements and cairns. The written message on this card to Miss J Campbell of Warrenhill Farm, Thankerton, reads, 'This is the 2nd herd's house and a miles up this hill is the other herd's house. The master fell in with a very severe accident last night which might cost him his life yet. The pony jammed him between the van and the wall and he has to go through an operation tomorrow'. John Buchan's mysterious novel, *Witchwood*, derived its name from the wood here between the west bank of the Tweed and the A701.

Above: Nothing remains of the old mill which was at the foot of the hill below Broughton House. The mill was fed by a lade which led to a mill pond behind the mill building. The hollow of the mill pond can still be seen. In 1881, James Ballantyne, who was then 80, was the miller, and his two daughters were dressmakers. John Plenderleith took over from him in the 1880s before the mill closed down around the turn of the century and John took over the mill at Stobo. Farmers from all the estate farms had to bring their oats to the mill. The miller paid his dues to the laird in kind.

Railway cottages (above) keep the same name to this day. Up to the early 1980s, the house across the street was also a shop, known as Thornbank Stores. The picture on the right shows Station Cottages before the road was straightened.

Broughton Station in 1905. The Symington-Biggar-Broughton line opened on November 5th 1860. Less than a year later, in August 1861, the company was taken over by the Caledonian Railway and the line was extended to Peebles in 1864, with intermediate stations at Lyne and Stobo. The arrival of the railway meant the end of the coaching inns, like The Green and The Crook at Tweedsmuir. The Green continued as a substantial farm, while other places, like the Crook Inn, reinvented themselves for the tourist trade. From here, meat went to London and milk to Edinburgh, as well as fleeces, potatoes, hay, rabbits and timber from the Rachan sawmills. The Peebles - Symington line was closed to passengers on 6 June 1950, the Peebles West to Broughton closed on 7 June 1954, and the Symington to Broughton line on 4 April 1966. When the passenger line was closed, an extra carriage was added to the goods train (known to the schoolchildren as the 'slaughterhouse train') to transport pupils to and from Peebles High School. Between Broughton and Biggar, the line is now used as a footpath. A coal yard occupies the derelict station site.

The Caledonian Railway train, hauled by locomotive No. 33, gets steam up to leave Broughton for Biggar c. 1904. Built by Neilson and Co in 1872, it had 7ft 2in coupled wheels. The locomotive itself was blue, with black chimney and smokebox, the buffer beam vermilion, the side frames crimson and the carriages reddish brown and white. These locomotives were built for secondary main line duties. No. 33 was designed by Benjamin Conner, built in 1872, renumbered 1033 in 1912 and withdrawn in 1915. Notice the 'hoop' the signalman is holding. This was part of a vital procedure on single-track lines. On the hoop is a pouch containing a metal tablet, which the driver had to receive from the signalman before leaving the station. Once the signalman had withdrawn the tablet at Broughton, no train from Biggar could be signalled on to the same stretch of line as the signals, points and tablet apparatus were all interlinked.

Left to right: Jane Robertson, ?, Mrs Susan Buchan, John Buchan, John Robertson outside the farmhouse at Fruid in the 1930s. John Robertson was the farm manager at Fruid, as his father had been before him. John Buchan (1875-1940), novelist, historian, statesman, was the son of a Presbyterian minister and Helen Masterton of The Green in Broughton. As a novelist, he is best known for his adventure stories, many of which recall the landscape of upper Tweeddale where he spent many idyllic childhood holidays, but he was also a writer of history and biography. Following a wartime career in Intelligence, he became a Member of Parliament in 1927. In 1935, he was made a peer and, as Baron Tweedsmuir, accepted the appointment to become Governor General of Canada, a country which he described as "simply Scotland on an extended scale'. He died there in 1940.

The main building, seen here in the early 1900s, has stood the test of time, although the school is now much extended. This building, erected in 1875, became the gym hall when the extension was added in 1937. Until the mid 20th century, it was a combined primary and secondary school.

Broughton School cup winners in 1936.
Standing (left to right) : George Howitt, J Morrison
Seated (left to right): David Whitefield, William Burnett, William Moir

Broughton

The school building and school house can be seen on the right of this picture of Manse Road in the early 1900s. Tennis courts and a bowling green now occupy the flat field beside it on land gifted by E B Masterton in 1925. The old manse, now called Easter Calzeat, was built in a flat, boggy area at the south-eastern end of this road in 1815. Rev Hamilton Paul chose the site which was described as 'the centre of a morass that could not be drained'. Despite protests from the presbytery, Rev Hamilton Paul persisted, as there was a large gravel bed in the middle of the marshland which has kept the house flood-free for almost two centuries!

RECREATION GROUND, BROUGHTON.

In the Middle Ages, the lands of Rachan belonged to the Geddes family, the earliest recorded proprietor being Andrew of Geddes, a burgess of Peebles in the 16th century. The original peel tower house is marked on Blaeu's map(1645) as Kattilhall. Traces of it could still be seen in the 19th century. In 1592, James Geddes of Glenhighton was murdered by the Tweedies, perhaps because he had married Margaret Veitch of Dawyck, the daughter of their sworn enemies. The Tweedies had 'stalked' him in Edinburgh for over a week, before shooting him in the back while he was having his horse's shoe renewed in the Cowgait. John Loch, a keen 'improver', who bought the estate in 1752, planted it with many fine trees. The next owner, Thomas Tweedie, a doctor with the East India Company, built the house above, landscaping the grounds with two ornamental lakes, stocked with trout. During the Second World War, the house became a convalescent home for servicemen. Henry Brown Marshall, who had large interests in South Africa, bought Rachan in 1897. Marshalltown, until recently the financial quarter of Johannesburg, was named after him.

In 1214, William Purvoys of 'Mospennoc' gave the Melrose monks right of way across his lands to Hopecarton. In 1524, the Tweedies and the Biggar Flemings were at loggerheads, because both families wanted offspring to marry Katherine Fraser, heiress of Fruid. Their rivalry culminated in John, Lord Fleming's murder, in Kilbucho Glen. His son, Malcolm was taken prisoner. In response, the Flemings brought an 'Indenture of Assythment' (similar to a legal demand for compensation) against them, and the Tweedies had to appear at Peebles, where they bound themselves to be servants of the Flemings and had to appear at Peebles Cross, *'in their lynning clathes, viz., sark alane, and yair thai haif offerit their naykit swords to the said Malcolm, his kyn and friendis'**. In return for Katherine's agreement to marry John Tweedie, Malcolm Fleming was released and awarded her possessions in Glenholm parish, part of which was Mossfennan. In the 17th century, Grizel Scott, heiress to Mossfennan, was pursued by three suitors. According to a contemporary ballad, Grizel was less attractive than her dowry:

> *'If ye be the leddy o this house,*
> *That we hae come sae far to see,*
> *There's many a servant lass in our country side*
> *That far exceeds the lady of the Logan Lee.'*

* *'in their linen clothes, viz. shirts only (i.e. without armour), and there they have offered their naked swords to the said Malcolm, his kin and friends'*

Picturesque Stobo station, which closed in 1950, is now a private house. The grassed over embankment and a trace of the old platform are still visible. Left of this picture was the core part of the dispersed community of Stobo; some parts of the old buildings were demolished to make way for the station and line.

The Stobo Express is ready to leave for Peebles. For over 20 years, from the 1880s into the 20th century, the station master was Malcolm Beaton from Snizort in the Isle of Skye. He and his family lived in the Station House, and several platelayers, a surfaceman and porter all lived in the village.

This row of houses was built when part of the old buildings across the road from them were demolished to make way for the new station in 1864. They are still known as 'Newhouses' and the hedge now practically hides them from the road. The picture was taken c. 1908. In the 1901 census, four families lived in Newhouses. Gabriel Anderson, the blacksmith, had lived there for over 20 years and Christina, one of his three daughters, was the sub postmistress. The post office, after being relocated several times, finally closed in 1987. John Anderson, who lived farther down the row, was also a blacksmith, with two apprentices. The head of the Hill household, Arthur, who had also lived there for over 20 years, was a coachman and Robert Milnes, head of the fourth family, was a joiner. Across the road, the former smithy, still operating in the 1940s, and wright's premises still exist, the latter now occupied by a silversmith.

Stobo Castle in 1912. The site of Stobo was originally known as Hillhouse, which would have been the laird's tower. In 1765, the then Lord Advocate James Montgomery purchased the Stobo lands after the previous laird, Sir David Murray, had lost it to the Crown. Sir David, only 20 years old, joined the '45 rebellion, taking with him Stobo Kirk's silver communion plate to help the cause. After Culloden, he escaped to the Highlands, only to be captured and condemned to death and his estates forfeited. Because of his youth, his sentence was commuted to exile in France, where he died in 1770. Sir James Montgomery was an 'improver', the first person to grow turnips in Tweeddale and the first in Scotland to use the two-horse plough. Apparently he was also very generous and paid the fines of poachers rather than let their families suffer. His son James, who succeeded him in 1803, built Stobo Castle. The architects of this baronial style building with its turrets and battlements were J & A Elliot of Edinburgh. It took six years (1805-1811), to build and was paid for by a legacy of £20,000 from the Duke of Queensberry. Sir James represented Peeblesshire in Parliament for 31 years until his death in 1839, but never made a single speech.

When Sir James Montgomery died (1839), his son Sir Graham Graham Montgomery took over. He too represented Peeblesshire in parliament. In the 1868 election, his majority was three votes and he had to flee from Peebles when his coach was attacked. Next time, he lost his seat. He died in 1901 and, when his son died the following year when he fell from a night express to London, two lots of death duties crippled the estate and it was sold to Mr Hylton Philipson. He created two lakes on the Stobo Burn and filled them with trout. The picture shows the 22 ft waterfall which descends from the lower lake to a Japanese water garden. When the Winyard family bought the castle in 1975, it had been empty for almost a decade and rampant with woodworm and dry rot. The Winyards converted the castle into a health spa, which opened in 1978 for a maximum of 26 guests. Today, the spa accommodates 100 residents as well as day visitors. In today's advertising brochure, the water gardens are said to 'promote a Zen-like calm'. Around 1850, embankments to reduce flooding were built from Crownhead to Burnfoot by Sir Graham Graham Montgomery. The problem of flooding was much reduced, following the creation of the Talla dam. In 1895 the Tweed froze over after ten weeks of frost that started about New Year 1895. Curlers had a game on the ice after sending the bachelors out first to test if it was safe!

Across the Tweed from Stobo Village is Dawyck Mill Farm: the mill pond no longer exists. Farther up the Lour Valley, there is Lour Farm, also part of the Dawyck estate since 1543. The Lour Valley is one of the parts of the upper Tweed which guards its secrets. 600 metres to the south-east of Dawyck Mill, there are the remains of an Iron Age fort whose ramparts and ditches were levelled to make way for a medieval village with a small tower house and associated buildings. In the First World War, 120 German prisoners of war were kept in wooden huts at Lour Farm. They worked as forestry labourers and in the saw mills. The most northerly headwater of the Lour is named chillingly 'Dead Wife's Burn'. Parallel to it, runs the old drove road across the grouse moors to the Manor Valley. On average, around 700 brace of grouse were shot in a season in the early 20th century.

This is the oldest church in Peeblesshire and was the 'mother church' of the district, dedicated to St Mungo. The whole barony of Stobo was owned by the see of Glasgow and under the jurisdiction of Glasgow cathedral, from at least the early 12th century. In the registers of the Archbishopric of Glasgow, there is a list of persons who are of ecclesiastical note in the area, among them Mihhyn the son of Edred at Stobo, Gillecrist the son of Bridoc at Kyngeldores, Cristin the hermit at Kyngledores, Adam and Cosouold the sons of Muryn at Oliver Castle. There have been several notable curates. At the end of the 15th century, curate John Reid was simply known as 'Stobo'. King James III provided him with an annuity of £20 for writing letters to the pope and 'sundry kings, princes and magnates beyond our kingdom'. It is probable that John Reid is the same 'gud gentil Stobo' mentioned in William Dunbar's 'Lament for the Makars'. Post Reformation, Stobo became the property of the Regent Earl of Morton in 1577. His tenure was short-lived as he was beheaded in the Grassmarket in Edinburgh in 1581 for his part in Lord Darnley's murder. Ironically, he was beheaded by the 'Maiden', the guillotine he himself had introduced into Scotland. The 12th century church was a simple rectangular nave, with a square chancel and perhaps a tower. The 15th century north transept chapel was reconstructed, mistakenly, in 1928 as a hermit's cell. The south porch is 15th/16th century. Grooves in the porch are said to have been made by children sharpening their slate pencils when the church was used as a school. Another theory suggests the grooves were made by the sharpening of arrowheads during the archery practice after church, which was compulsory after the defeat at the Battle of Flodden. After the Reformation, the fine mouldings in the interior were covered with plaster, other ornate corners were covered up and jougs attached to the front porch. In 1863, Sir Graham Graham Montgomery paid for the church's restoration and two boarded up Norman windows and a tomb were uncovered. In the 1970s, during new central heating installation, old graves were found beneath the floor.

The old manse (*above*) is now a private house, B listed, known as 'The Glebe'. In 1882, Robert Louis Stevenson spent two weeks at Stobo Manse. During this visit, he wrote a comic poem about the place to the poet and critic, Edmund Gosse:

"I would shoot you, but I have no bow:
The place is not called Stobs but Stobo.
As Gallic kids complain of 'bobo'*,
I mourn for your mistake of Stobo"

* French term for a **Bo**urgeois **Bo**hemian

Drumelzier in 1915. A witness to a document of *c.* 1200 is recorded as living in 'Dunmedler'. While 'Dun' is Gaelic for a fort, the 'medler' part is more elusive, but may mean 'of the warriors'. While the earliest known proprietors were the Frasers, the most notorious were certainly the Tweedies, who were entrenched in various strongholds throughout upper Tweeddale, but had their main headquarters in Drumelzier. They first settled here around the 14th century, having obtained land from the Frasers to which they added by judicious marriages. By the end of the 15th century, they had become one of the most powerful families in Peeblesshire, with tight control over the upper Tweed Valley, having built their towers at strategic points where they could 'levy' payment from travellers crossing their territory. The story goes that one day they accosted a traveller to demand tribute – but the traveller turned out to be King James V, who took appropriate retribution.

Drumelzier in 1904, looking north. The miniature 'table mountain' on the right is Tinnis Castle, one of the main Tweedie fortresses. Tin/Din/Dun/Tinnis are all variatons of the same word, meaning 'fort'. Tinnis Castle was built in the 15th-16th century, but its origins go back more than 2000 years as it was built inside an Iron Age fort. Traces of the Iron Age ramparts and ditches can still be found and there are Iron Age cultivation terraces on the north west slope. The medieval castle was built in a quadrangle with the living quarters on the SE side, probably in a tower. From the widely scattered debris remaining, it has been deduced that the castle was blown up, perhaps by the Flemings in revenging the murder of John in 1524. The other theory that Tinnis was blown up by King James VI in 1592 is largely discredited, as the king's demolition order was in fact for 'Tynneis' in Selkirkshire.

Drumelzier Castle, also built by the Tweedies, is now just a pile of rubble within the precincts of Drumelzier Place Farm. The walls were 3-4 feet thick and the towers were three storeys high, with an attic. Violence of every variety permeates the Tweedie history. They plundered cattle, accosted travellers, two of them were implicated in the murder of Rizzio in 1566 and, in 1565, Adam Tweedie cut off the 'luggis' of Robert Ramage. The most lawless was probably James, who lived in the second half of the 16th century. For various crimes, he 'did time' in the Tolbooth in Edinburgh and Linlithgow. In 1590, a gang of Tweedies murdered Patrick Veitch of Dawyck at Neidpath Castle 'with swordis and pistolettes cruellie and unmercifullie'. In revenge, the Veitches killed John Tweedie in Edinburgh. James himself met a violent end, killed in single combat by the laird of Dawyck in 1612. His son James fell into debt and Lord Hay of Yester obtained the lands and barony of Drumelzier in 1632. The Hay family lived in Drumelzier Castle for the next 200 years.

Drumelzier Haugh is one of the widest parts of the valley floor in upper Tweeddale, providing both pasture land and, farther from the river flood plain, arable. James Affleck, born here in 1776, was a rural poet, whose work describes life at the end of the 18th century. His grandfather had made a living from catching fish in the Tweed and selling them. At the age of 8, James himself was employed herding the cows by the river, later as a gadboy, who guided the horses that pulled the old Scots plough. Up to the end of the 18th century, Drumelzier was a ferm-toun, where the strips of arable land (rigs) were worked in common and the hill grazing used as common pasture. The Agricultural Revolution put an end to that system as the Haugh was consolidated into 300 acres of arable land. The Lowland Clearances which followed saw the number of houses in the village and the population of the parish as a whole decrease by more than 50%. In 1790, there were 26 houses in Drumelzier; in 1834, only 15. Up to the late 18th century, most of Drumelzier's workers were shepherds, cowherds, ploughmen and farm servants. In 1790, there were also four tailors, two masons and two smiths. By 1834, it was a village of tenant farmers and a single weaver.

In the Peeblesshire Ordnance Survey name book (1856-58) it is recorded that the school was built in 1821 and that the average attendance was 24, twelve boys and twelve girls. The teacher was Mr. William Paterson, who was also responsible for providing the data for the Ordnance Survey records. In the same account, the village is described as follows: 'A small Irregular Village on the East Side of the River Tweed on the Drummelzier Burn. It Consists of the Parish Church, Manse and School, a corn Mill, Smithy and Several Cottages Mostly thatched but in good Repairs' Up to 1900, only the manse, schoolhouse and millhouse had a water supply. The village water, which came from a spring near Tinnis Castle, was drawn from a spout outside the smiddy.

Merlin's grave, near the confluence of the Tweed and Powsail. The thorn bush marks where Merlin lies buried. But which Merlin? The Merlin of Arthurian legend is confused with Myrddin (Welsh for Merlin) Caledonis a 6th century pagan prophet. After a battle near Carlisle, when the pagan forces were defeated by the new Christian ones, Myrddin lost his leader, his nephew and his mind and became a gaunt, crazed wanderer. The story goes that, wandering in the Drumelzier hills, he met St Kentigern who converted him to Christianity and baptised him. That same day, he was attacked by a gang of local shepherds who pushed him over a cliff into the Powsail where he was impaled by a stake in the river bed before he drowned – and Merlin had predicted he would have a triple death; by falling, stabbing and drowning. Another old prophecy read, 'When Tweed and Powsail meet at Merlin's grave, Scotland and England shall one monarch have'. On the day James VI was crowned joint monarch of Scotland and England, this unique event occurred when the Tweed overflowed its banks and joined the Powsail where Merlin is allegedly buried. The only archaeological discovery made in situ was a Bronze Age cist. In Stobo Church, a stained glass window depicts Merlin's baptism. Part of the altar stone where St Kentigern was said to have converted him is in the church.

Drumelzier

Although Drumelzier Church has changed little since 1906, the massive restorations that took place, particularly in the early 18th century, have obliterated most signs of the original building. The small belfry on the western gable dates from the 17th or 18th century and there is a 17th century Tweedie burial vault at the east end. Above the door there is a modern panel which bears the words, 'THOL AND THINK', the ironic motto of the Tweedie family whose members were not noted for either activity! Indeed, the first post Reformation minister, the Rev Thomas Bissett, noted in 1567 that the Tweedies' terrorist tendancies were preventing people from attending church as they were afraid to venture anywhere.' In the Disruption of 1843, the Rev James Somerville, with about 20 members of his congregation, seceded to join the Free Church at Broughton. However, one of the Tweedie lairds was generous enough to provide a manse in 1598, but the building was so poor it was a ruin by 1650.

The Dawyck estate is one of the hidden jewels of Tweeddale. This is Dawyck House *c.* 1912. The name Dawyck first appears in the 13th century: the Norman William Le Vache swore fealty to Edward I in 1296. From Le Vache, came the name Veitch. The Veitches owned the lands of Dawyck from at least the early 15th century until debts forced them to sell in the late 18th century. They feuded constantly with the Tweedies, but were not by any means innocent victims. In the 15th century, William Veitch was a notorious cattle robber and another William Veitch, also a reiver, in the 16th century, was known as the Deil o Dawyck because he had great strength and no one he felled with his sword ever got up. James Naesmyth of Posso acquired Dawyck in 1691. His son, also Sir James Naesmythe (1704-1779), was a pupil of the renowned Swedish botanist, Carl Linnaeus, and Sir James himself is described as a 'famous botanist' in the records of Padua University in 1753. He planted the first larches in Scotland at Dawyck in 1725. The Balfours who succeeded the Naysmythes carried on the botanical work. Colonel F R S Balfour planted one ton of daffodils every year for 20 years and the snowdrops along the burn were planted by a Drumelzier girl, Agnes Blackstocks, who was a laundrymaid at the end of the 19th century. Herons have always lived at Dawyck and there is a record that James IV received a gift of herons from Dawyck in 1497. Allexander Pennecuik, who wrote *A Historical Description of the Shire of Tweeddale* in 1715, describes 'Here in an Old Orch-yard did the herons in my time build their Nests upon some large Pear trees, whereupon in the Harvest time are to be seen much Fruit growing, and Trouts and Iles (eels) crawling down the body of these Trees. These fish the Herons take out of the River of Tweed to their Nests, and as they go in at the Mouth, so they are seen to squirt out again at the Draught. And this is the remarkable Riddle they so much talk off, to have Flesh, Fish, and Fruit at the same time upon one Tree.' Although this curious phenomenon can no longer be seen, Dawyck Gardens, now part of the Royal Botanic Garden Edinburgh, are still a place of botanical wonder. Research and conservation are also carried out and there is a programme of science and education activities.

The Manor Valley

People have lived in the Manor Valley since the Stone Age, and the landscape resonates with the mystery of their lives and deaths. Names like Posso, Macbeth's Castle, Saint Gordian, Horse-hope-shank, Bellanrig, Hundleshope, Bitch Craig demand exploration. According to W J Watson, the names Manor and Posso both imply the residence of a chieftain, but the origins of many of the names, as well as the remains, can only be guessed at. In many ways, the Manor Valley is a distillation of the quiet and unquiet mystique of the upper Tweed Valley.

The Bellanridge standing stone was moved from its original site at Bellanridge Farm and built into this drystane dyke. It is over six feet tall and pitted with natural hollows, which at one time were mistaken for cup and ring markings.

St Gordian's Cross, on the lower slopes of Posso craig, west of Kirkhope, is said to mark the site of St Gordian's kirk, but archaeologists are fairly certain that none of the remains of buildings on the site are those of a church. Similarly, the so-called font stone at its base is not a font stone, but a cross base, the socket of which has been enlarged to form a rough basin. There is also confusion about the saint, whether Gordian or Gorgon, and as there are two of each, all 4th century martyrs, the identity remains an ecclesiastical mystery.

The name Hallyards is first mentioned in a document of 1559. The original part of the present dwelling, probably a tower house, is the rectangular area in the south-east, which has four symmetrically set windows. The second storey and the bow front were added at the end of the 18th century. Preserved in the stonework is a lintel engraved 'IS HG 1647', the initials of John Scott and Helen Geddes who were married in 1635. On a visit to Hallyards in 1797, Sir Walter Scott met David Ritchie, the inspiration for his novel, *The Black Dwarf*. Andrew Clason of Hallyards, who died in 1850 is noted for two things. He commissioned the Black Dwarf statue, which was set up on the Hallyards lawn, and which was carried from Leith by seven horses. He also introduced the white hare, the first of which he released at Bitch Craig in the upper reaches of the Manor Valley.

This is the home of David Ritchie, known as 'The Black Dwarf'. He was 3 feet 6 inches tall. The original cottage, built by David's own hands, no longer exists. This house, photographed in the 1950s, was built for David in 1802 by Sir James Naysmyth. Alongside the ordinary entrance is a 4 foot high one for David. His sister, who lived next door, was never allowed inside his house as they were not on friendly terms. David died in 1811, leaving £20 in bags of silver coins, half of which his sister had to return to the church Poor Fund which had supported him throughout his life.

Statue of the Black Dwarf. It is generally agreed that the statue is more caricature that representation. In fact, David's feet were so mis-shapen, he wrapped them in rags as it would have been impossible for him to wear any kind of shoes. David Ritchie was known in Manor as 'Bowed Davie of the Wuddus'(Woodhouse), where he lived. Born in Stobo parish *c.* 1740, he had the head and torso of a fully-grown man, with very long muscular arms. His legs, however, were severely deformed, described by a 19th century Peebles surgeon, as 'bent like cork-screws', so that he walked on the inside of his ankles and his knees were crossed over. For two years, he worked at Broughton Mill, stirring the husks of oats. After a brief sojourn in Edinburgh where he had been sent to learn the trade of brushmaking and where he suffered much unwanted attention and ridicule, he came to live in the Manor Valley, where he built himself a house and garden. He kept bees, grew medicinal herbs and loved flowers, animals and beautiful women, to whom he occasionally presented a flower from his garden. Despite a very limited education, Davie was able to read. According to Dr John Brown, he enjoyed the poet Allan Ramsay, but hated Burns. He wore a red cowl like a nightcap and walked with a long pole for support. Despite his infirmity, he used to walk to Peebles and back regularly, a round trip of eight miles. Although he was supported by the Poor Fund, the local people supplied him with provisions, perhaps because they were a little afraid of his alleged supernatural powers and his occasional violence.

David had expressed the wish to be buried at the top of Woodhill with a rowan tree alongside to ward off witches. However, he was buried in Manor Kirkyard but, according to Dr John Brown, there had been a rumour circulating that his body had been removed by body-snatchers. When his sister died in 1821, the grave-diggers looked for his bones and found them still in situ. They removed them to Woodhouse and they eventually came into the hands of Andrew Ballantyne of Woodhouse, but who knows where their last resting place is? This is a memorial stone – with David's wished-for rowan tree beside it.

The Manor Valley

Left: Barns is one of a chain of peel towers in the Manor Valley, carefully sited so that beacon warnings from one to the other could be easily seen. The tower was built by the Burnets, who came to Manor from Broughton in the 15th century and remained there for over 300 years. Tradition has it that the 16th century William Burnet, known as 'The Hoolet' because of his keen night vision, lived to be 107. His grandson, heavily in debt to the earl of Traquair who was anxious to expand his territory and influence in Peeblesshire, had to mortgage the estate. This obviously caused him considerable angst as he was accused of storming into Peebles by night, terrifying the citizens with his threats and 'mutilating with his sword' the watch's hand. His son tried to clear the debt, but died of wounds at the Battle of Steinkirk, leaving no children, so that the estate passed to a cousin, who did manage to rescind the mortgage. James, the last Burnet of Barns, is credited with introducing shorthorn cattle. Like the Traquair earls, the Burnets were staunch Jacobites.

Above: Castlehill Tower, built at the end of the 15th century, sits on a rocky hillock on the west bank of the Manor Water, commanding the ford on the old road to Hundleshope. It was built by the Lowis family, who lived there until 1629. After leaving Manor and indeed Scotland, members of the Lowis family continued to add Menar (Manor) to their title. Wilhelm von Lowis of Menar was a Colonel in the army of the great Swedish King Gustavus Adolphus. One of his descendants, Friedrich von Lowis of Menar, commanded the Russian army for a time in 1813 and present-day descendants live in Berlin.